Hummingbirds

tiny but MIGHTY

by Julianne Gehman and Illustrated by Patricia Gehman

I'm Ruby, a ruby-throated hummingbird.

I am a bird so tiny I can sit in a teaspoon.

You can hardly see my wings
because I move them so fast.

I can fly upside down, backwards
and even hover like a helicopter.

Hey! There goes Rube!
He's headed for the feeder.
Got to head him off.

The people in the house say,
"Why can't they share?
There are enough feeding spots."

But they don't get it. The fun
is fighting for a spot.

We travel from flower to flower: trumpet creeper, scarlet sage, bee-balm, red morning-glory.

We eat lots of sugar-water or nectar to give us the energy we need. After all, our wings beat 55 to 75 times each second. Isn't that amazing?

We eat more than our
body weight daily.

How much do you weigh?

Do you think you could eat
that much food in a day?

Our legs and feet are so small we cannot walk on the ground.

We sit on thin branches and wires and sing, "Look at me... Tee tee tee tee tee!"

But we don't want
everyone to see us.

We have enemies like hawks
and frogs and cats.
There are other dangers too.

We may get caught in a
spider's web or trapped in a
garage. Garage door emergency
handles look like one of our
favorite red flowers. Once
inside a garage, we fly upward
and hit the ceiling again and
again often hurting ourselves.

We boys don't pay attention to
girl hummingbirds until
nesting season.

Then we are acrobats, attracting
them with our bright colors
(We are prettier than the girls!)
as we make big, swooping dives.

We spend summers in
North America and Canada.

When days begin to get
shorter, we head south.

Before we leave, we have
to eat and eat and eat.
We need plenty of energy
to fly as far as Mexico
and Central America.

We may fly over the Gulf of Mexico. That's more than 500 miles non-stop.

We are hummingbirds...
tiny but MIGHTY!

Hummingbird facts

Hummingbirds get their name from the whirring sound their wings make as they fly.

The ruby-throated hummingbird spends spring and summer in Northeastern United States. It is the male whose throat reflects the bright red colored. Ruby-throated hummingbirds are just one kind, or species, of hummingbird.

There are over 300 species of hummingbirds living in North, Central and South America. Most of them (about 95%) live south of the United States.

Different species of hummingbirds have different colors and some, like the ruby-throated, are named for their colors—the violet-crowned, blue-throated, buff-bellied, white-eared, and black-chinned, for instance. Some others are named for the people who first saw them, like Allen's, Anna's and Costa's.

Most of the hummingbird's diet is nectar they drink from flowers. They depend on the flowers and the flowers depend on them. As they feed, they pollinate thousands of plants. Pollen sticks to their long breaks and is deposited on the next flower they visit.

Hummingbird facts

Hummingbirds may also eat some insects and, or rare occasions, insects like the praying mantis may catch them off guard and eat them.

The mother hummingbird builds the nest and cares for the young. The male's job is to defend their territory. Male hummingbirds are fierce little fighters and may even attack hawks, deadly enemies, by maneuvering around them. They can fly up, down, sideways and even upside down to get at the intruder.

Hummingbirds an be quite tame, too, drinking from colorful dishes that people patiently hold. They will visit your feeders if you fill them regularly and change the sugar water every few days to keep it fresh.

Search the web and you will find much more interesting information about this beautiful, feisty little bird.

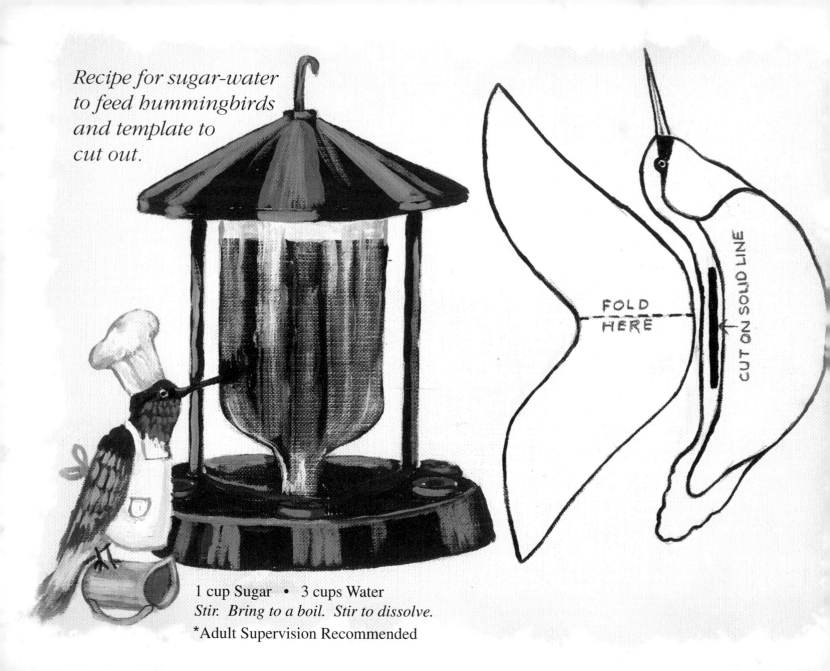

Recipe for sugar-water to feed hummingbirds and template to cut out.

FOLD HERE

CUT ON SOLID LINE

1 cup Sugar • 3 cups Water

Stir. Bring to a boil. Stir to dissolve.

*Adult Supervision Recommended